SIGNS of GRACE™

You Are Loved

Preparing for First Holy Communion

Student Activity Book

This belongs to:

_____

AUGUSTINE INSTITUTE
UNDERSTAND, LIVE, AND SHARE YOUR FAITH

Writers: Paul McCusker, Ashley Crane, Mary Pollice, Patricia Morris, Linda Platt (Spanish translator)
Print Production/Graphic Design: Jeff Cole, Brenda Kraft, Grace Hagan, Julia DeLapp, Emily Lehman, Mackenzie Key, Ann Diaz
Layout and Design: Ben Dybas, Christina Gray, Mike Fontecchio, Kirk Flory, Jane Myers, Denise Fath
Media: Steve Flanigan, Justin Leddick, Kevin Mallory, Ted Mast, Jon Ervin
Contributors: Professor Lucas Pollice, Dr. Ben Akers, Dr. Mark Giszczak, Dr. Tim Gray, Fr. John Riley
Reviewers: Constance Graves, Dr. Scott Helefinger, Dr. Elizabeth Klein, Morgan McGinn, Jennifer McCullum, Monica Metz, Sister Marie Dominique Mullen, Ann McPherson, Lorie Pritchard, Mary Pollice, Sister Dominic Quinn, Alicia Riggs, Karol Sydel, Natalie Travis
Images and Photographs: Provided by Augustine Institute, Robert Dunn/Advocate Art, Gabrielle Schadt, Restored Traditions, Shutterstock.com. Used with permission.

Augustine Institute
6160 South Syracuse Way, Suite 310
Greenwood Village, CO 80111
Information: 303-937-4420
AugustineInstitute.org
TheSignsofGrace.org

Printed in Canada
ISBN 978-0-9991778-2-2

Introduction to Family Take-Home Pages

Our true happiness comes from God—and it is through God's gift of the family that we first learn about our Catholic Faith and experience the joy of life with Christ. Taking time to pray with your family, going to Mass together, receiving the sacraments...all of these practices give us the grace to live a holy life.

One important way families can grow closer to God and to each other is by reading the Bible together. God speaks to us each time we read Scripture!

Family Prayer with Lectio Divina: A Way to Read Scripture

Lectio divina is an ancient practice of prayer based on God's Word. It is our hope that using these simple steps as you study the Scriptures with your child will help you to incorporate God's Word into your daily lives.

Here is a brief description of each step:

1. Sacred Reading of the Scriptures: Read and reread the Scripture, paying close attention to words, details, themes, and patterns that speak to you.

2. Meditation: Reflect on what you read to understand the meaning. Allow the Holy Spirit to guide you as you spend time thinking about what you have read.

3. Prayer: Bring your reflections and thoughts to God in prayer. Talk to God about how your meditation on the Scripture affects your life and the lives of those around you.

4. Contemplation: Quietly rest and listen to God's voice. Be patient as you practice this step and try to be open to God's voice speaking into your life.

5. Resolution: This is a call to action, inviting you to respond to what you read in Scripture and prayed about and to put what you learned into practice.

Take time to follow these simple steps with your child. This will provide a way to review the week's Scripture verses while learning a beautiful method for praying with the Scriptures—a method practiced by the saints for centuries!

Introducción a Páginas de Tarea para la Familia

Nuestra verdadera felicidad viene de Dios, y la familia es el primer lugar donde aprendemos nuestra fe y experimentamos la vida con Cristo. Recibimos la gracia para vivir una vida santa cuando tomamos tiempo para orar con nuestra familia, cuando vamos a misa juntos y recibimos los sacramentos.

Una manera en que las familias pueden acercarse a Dios y entre sí, es leyendo la Biblia juntos. ¡Dios nos habla cada vez que leemos la Sagrada Escritura!

Un Resumen de Lectio Divina

Lectio divina es una práctica antigua para mejorar la vida de oración de una persona, por medio del poder de la Palabra de Dios. Esperamos que al usar estos pasos simples mientras estudias las Escrituras con tu hijo, desarrolles una forma eficaz de llenarte de la Palabra de Dios.

Ésta es una breve descripción de cada paso:

1. Lectura Sagrada de la Escritura: La lectura (y relectura) de la Sagrada Escritura, prestando atención a las palabras, detalles, temas y patrones que hablen a tu corazón.

2. Meditación: La meditación o reflexión de lo que se ha leído para entenderlo mejor. Es permitirle al Espíritu Santo que te guíe, mientras tomas un tiempo pensando en lo que has leído.

3. Oración: Un tiempo para llevar nuestros pensamientos meditados a Dios en la oración. Hablar con Dios sobre cómo las conexiones e implicaciones de tu meditación de la Escritura afectan tu vida y la de los que te rodean.

4. Contemplación: Un tiempo de silencio y descanso, cuando escuchamos la voz de Dios. Ten paciencia mientras practicas este paso y luchas por ser receptivo a la voz de Dios que te está hablando en tu vida.

5. Resolución: Un llamado a tomar una resolución y acción, invitándonos a responder a las cosas que hemos leído en la Sagrada Escritura.

Toma tiempo para seguir estos pasos simples con tu hijo. Esto te proveerá una forma de repasar los pasajes de las Escrituras de la semana, así como ayudarte a enseñar a tu hijo un método hermoso de orar con la Sagrada Escritura—¡un método practicado por los santos por siglos!

Each weekly Family Take-Home Page will include these sections:

✓ Things We Learned This Week

Review the weekly Bible verses, which we'll include here, with your child. Set aside time with your child each week to read through the verses together and practice *lectio divina*. Talk about what these verses mean to you and ask what they mean to your child. Brainstorm ways you can put the verses into practice in your everyday lives.

Let's Talk About It

Look for these weekly discussion-starter questions. Engage your child in conversation using these prompts to help reinforce what they learned in the week's lesson, and encourage them to put the lessons into practice in their lives.

Our Family Prays Together

Spend time together with this weekly prayer. Help your child develop a habit of prayer during this important formative time.

Family Fun Activity!

We'll include a short activity that you can do with your child. Use this time to reinforce the lesson and unite as a family of faith.

Explore the Faith Together

For more information on Catholic traditions and teachings as well as Catholic movies, books, audios, and more, please check out formed.org. Ask your Director of Religious Education if your parish has a subscription to log on for free!

Cada Página de Tarea para la Familia (una por semana) incluirá estas secciones:

☑ Lo que aprendimos esta semana

Repasa los versículos semanales de la Biblia con tu hijo, que incluiremos en esta sección. Toma tiempo con tu hijo cada semana para leer los versículos juntos y practiquen *lectio divina*.

Platica sobre lo que estos versículos significan para ti y pregúntale a tu hijo lo que significan para él/ella. Saquen ideas en que puedan poner esos versículos en práctica en sus vidas diarias.

Hablemos Sobre Esto

Busca estas preguntas semanales para iniciar una conversación. Platica con tu hijo usando estas preguntas, para ayudar a reforzar lo que ya ha aprendido en la lección de la semana, y anímalo a ponerlos en práctica en su vida.

Oremos en Familia

Tomen un tiempo juntos para hacer esta oración semanal. Ayuda a tu hijo a desarrollar un hábito de oración durante este tiempo importante de formación.

¡Actividad Familiar Divertida!

Incluiremos una actividad pequeña que puedes hacer con tu hijo. Usa este tiempo para reforzar la lección y para unirse como familia de fe.

Exploren Juntos La Fe

Para más información acerca de las tradiciones y enseñanzas católicas, y para encontrar material católico como películas, libros, audios, etc., puedes checar la página formed.org. ¡Pregúntale al director de educación religiosa si tu parroquia tiene una suscripción parroquial para tener acceso gratuito!

Preparing the Way for Christ

☺ Connect — Opening Activity

God Saves His People

The Israelites were slaves in Egypt, so God sent Moses to tell Pharaoh to let God's people go! Place the stickers and color the picture.

Let's Live It

Preparing the World for Christ

Answer the clues below to complete the crossword puzzle.

WORD BANK

Manna

Passover

Plagues

Tabernacle

Pharaoh

Moses

Egypt

Israelites

ACROSS

1. The king of Egypt.

3. The man sent by God to lead the Israelites out of slavery in Egypt.

5. A large, beautiful tent where the presence of God dwelt.

6. The place where the Israelites were slaves.

DOWN

1. The special feast when the Israelites remember how God saved them.

2. God's special people.

3. In the desert God gave the Israelites bread from heaven to eat.

4. Ten bad things that happened to Egypt to convince Pharaoh to let God's people go.

Jesus Said,

"I am the bread of life. Your fathers ate manna in the wilderness.... I am the living bread which came down from heaven..."

—John 6:49, 51

The Presence of God

God was present to the Israelites in the desert in the pillar of cloud by day and the pillar of fire by night. Then, when the Israelites built the Tabernacle, the cloud of God's presence came and dwelt there. Today, Jesus is present in the Tabernacle you see in your church.

Write down on the lines below one way that God is present in your life. Then draw a picture of the Tabernacle you see at church.

_____

_____

_____

"The LORD went before them by day in a pillar of cloud to lead them along the way, and by night in a pillar of fire to give them light"

—Exodus 13:21

☑ Things We Learned This Week

1. God saved his people Israel by delivering them from slavery through the Passover event and by feeding them with manna in the desert.

2. Passover was one of the most important sacrifices for the Jewish people, and God wanted them to remember this saving event every year.

3. Sacrifice is offering something to God for the forgiveness of sin or in thanksgiving for God's great gifts. Jesus offered himself as a sacrifice so that our sins could be forgiven.

4. The most important way we offer sacrifice to God is by attending Mass.

5. Today every Catholic church has a Tabernacle where the Eucharist is reserved for prayer and adoration outside of Mass. Jesus is present in the Tabernacle.

◯ Let's Talk About It

1. **How is Christ like the Passover lamb in the Scripture story from Exodus 12:14–28?**

2. **Talk about how the Passover meal reminds us of the Eucharist we receive at the Holy Mass.**

3. **Discuss how wonderful it is that we can receive the Eucharist every Sunday at Mass, and try to think of one way you can make God's love present in your family or at your school.**

✝ Let's Read God's Word
The Feast of Passover

The Scripture reading for this week's lesson was from Exodus 12:14–28. Please take time to read and reflect on this passage as a family.

☑ Lo que aprendimos esta semana:

1. Dios salvó a Su pueblo Israel, liberándolo de la esclavitud por medio del evento pascual y alimentándolo con el maná en el desierto.

2. La Pascua fue el sacrificio más importante para el pueblo judío; Dios quiso que ellos recordaran este evento salvífico cada año.

3. Un sacrificio es cuando ofrecemos algo a Dios por el perdón de los pecados, o en acción de gracias por los dones que recibimos de Él. Jesús se ofrece a sí mismo en sacrificio para que nuestros pecados puedan ser perdonados.

4. La manera más importante en que ofrecemos sacrificio a Dios es asistiendo a Misa.

5. Hoy en día, cada iglesia Católica tiene un Tabernáculo, donde se reserva la Eucaristía para la oración y adoración en momentos fuera de la Misa. Jesús está presente en el Tabernáculo.

💬 ¡Hablemos Sobre Esto!

1. Haciendo referencia a este texto, ¿cómo muestra la historia que Cristo es como el Cordero Pascual?

2. Platiquen cómo el alimento pascual nos recuerda a la Eucaristía que recibimos en la Santa Misa.

3. Platiquen sobre qué maravilloso es que podamos recibir la Eucaristía cada domingo en la Misa, y traten de pensar en una forma en que puedan hacer el amor de Dios presente en su familia o en la escuela.

✝ Leamos la Palabra de Dios
La Fiesta de la Pascua

La lectura de la Sagrada Escritura para la lección de esta semana fue del libro de Éxodo 12:14–28. Por favor tomen tiempo para leer y reflexionar sobre este pasaje en familia.

Family Fun Activity ✏️

This week we are focusing on God's presence. A great idea to make God's presence felt in your home is to set up a family altar where you can all pray or just spend quiet time with the Lord. You can put a crucifix and a candle on it as well as a Bible or some flowers and a rosary. This should be a special place for your family, so make it your own.

Explore the Faith Together

For more information on Catholic traditions and teachings as well as Catholic movies, books, audios, and more, please check out formed.org. Ask your Director of Religious Education if your parish has a subscription to log on for free!

✋ Our Family Prays Together

The Morning Offering

Parent:

O my Jesus, I offer you my prayers, my work, and my play,

Response:

everything that makes me happy, and everything that makes me sad,

Parent:

in union with the Holy Sacrifice of the Mass all over the world,

Response:

for all the needs of my family and friends,

Parent:

and especially for the intentions of the Holy Father, the Pope.

Response:

Please prepare my heart to receive my First Holy Communion.

All:

Amen.

¡Actividad Familiar ✏️ Divertida!

Esta semana nos enfocaremos en la presencia de Dios. Una idea divertida para hacer sentir la presencia de Dios en tu hogar es acomodar un altar familiar donde todos puedan orar o simplemente pasar tiempo en silencio con el Señor. Pueden colocar ahí un crucifijo y una vela, así como una Biblia, algunas flores o un rosario. Se recomienda que este lugar sea un lugar especial para tu familia, entonces hazlo tuyo también.

Exploren Juntos La Fe

Para más información acerca de las tradiciones y enseñanzas católicas, y para encontrar material católico como películas, libros, audios, etc., puedes checar la página formed.org. ¡Pregúntale al director de educación religiosa si tu parroquia tiene una suscripción parroquial para tener acceso gratuito!

✋ ¡Oremos Juntos En Familia!

Ofrecimiento Matutino

Papá/Mamá:

Oh mi Jesús, te ofrezco mis oraciones, mi trabajo y mi juego,

Respuesta:

todo lo que me hace feliz y lo que me entristece,

Papá/Mamá:

en unión con el Santo Sacrificio de la Misa celebrada en todo el mundo,

Respuesta:

por todas las necesidades de mi familia y amigos,

Papá/Mamá:

y especialmente por las intenciones del Santo Padre, el Papa.

Respuesta:

Te pido que me ayudes a preparar mi corazón para recibir mi Primera Comunión.

Todos:

Amén.

♫ Let's Sing God's Praises

Go Down, Moses!

When Israel was in
   Egypt's land,
Let my people go;
[stomp, stomp, clap.]

Oppressed so hard they could
   not stand,
Let my people go.
[stomp, stomp, clap.]

(Chorus)

Go down, Moses,
Way down in Egypt's land;

Tell old Pharaoh
Let my people go!
[stomp, stomp, clap.]

"Thus says the Lord," bold
   Moses said,
Let my people go;
[stomp, stomp, clap.]

"If not, I'll smite your
   first-born dead,"
Let my people go.
[stomp, stomp, clap.]

(Chorus)

No more shall they in
   bondage toil,
Let my people go;
[stomp, stomp, clap.]

Let them come out with
   Egypt's spoil,
Let my people go.
[stomp, stomp, clap.]

(Chorus)

Words by H. T. Burleigh (1866–1949)
© 2018 Augustine Institute

10

Flash Cards

Key Words – Session 1

Moses	Plagues
Sacrifice	Unleavened bread
Passover	Israel

Flash Cards

Key Words – Session 1 (definitions)

A series of disasters that God brought upon Egypt.

An Israelite who God chose to deliver the nation of Israel from slavery.

Bread that is made without yeast so that it doesn't rise.

Offering of something to God for the forgiveness of sin or in thanksgiving for God's great gifts.

The nation that God chose to be his Chosen People.

The memorial that recalls how God saved his people from slavery and death in Egypt.

Flash Cards

Key Words – Session 1

Manna

Seder Meal

Flash Cards

Key Words – Session 1 (definitions)

A memorial meal that recalls the exodus of the Israelites from slavery in Egypt.

The bread from heaven that God gave to the Israelites in the desert.

The Last Supper

☺ Connect — Opening Activity

Jesus Institutes the Mass

At the Last Supper, Jesus said, "This is my body," and "This is my blood." This was the very first Mass! And the Apostles became the very first priests!

Place the stickers and color the picture.

Let's Live It

Jesus Gives Us the Priesthood

Jesus instituted the priesthood at the Last Supper. This means that the Apostles were the first priests of the Catholic Church. Jesus still works through your priest today. When your priest repeats Jesus's words and consecrates the bread and wine at Mass, they become the Body and Blood of Jesus.

Write a thank you note to your priest for the many ways he brings you closer to Jesus.

Dear Father,

_____

_____

_____

_____

_____

_____

Jesus Said,

"He who eats my flesh and drinks my blood has eternal life, and I will raise him up at the last day. For my flesh is food indeed, and my blood is drink indeed."

—John 6:54–55

Bread from Heaven

Jesus said that his Body is true food and his Blood is true drink. The Body and Blood of Christ in the Eucharist is true food for your soul. How does the Eucharist make your soul strong?

Write down some ways that the Eucharist helps your soul. Then draw a picture of how you think your soul will look when you receive the Eucharist.

_____

_____

_____

Jesus Said,

"I am the bread of life; he who comes to me shall not hunger, and he who believes in me shall never thirst."

—John 6:35

20

☑ Things We Learned This Week

1. The miracle of changing water into wine at the Wedding Feast at Cana shows that Jesus is God and points forward to the Eucharist.

2. At the Last Supper, Jesus institutes the Sacrament of the Eucharist.

3. Jesus tells the Apostles to continue to celebrate the Eucharist, and it is continued in the Church today in the Mass.

4. Real Presence means the reality that Jesus is truly present, Body, Blood, Soul, and Divinity, in the Eucharist.

5. When the priest says the Words of Consecration, "This is my Body," and "This is the chalice of my Blood," the bread and wine are changed into the Body and Blood of Christ.

6. Transubstantiation means that the bread and wine really change into Jesus's Body and Blood.

Q Let's Talk About It

1. How can we know that the bread and wine truly become the Body and Blood of Christ?

2. Talk about how we can become truly united to Jesus every time we go to Mass.

3. Discuss with your son or daughter how you felt when you first received Holy Communion. How was that day special and how was it life-changing?

✝ Let's Read God's Word
The Last Supper

The Scripture reading for this week's lesson was from Luke 22:14–20. Please take time to read and reflect on this passage as a family.

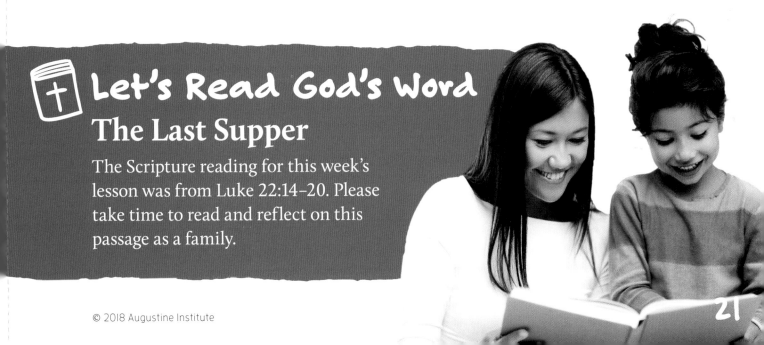

☑ Lo que aprendimos esta semana:

1. El milagro de cambiar agua en vino en las Bodas en Caná pone de manifiesto que Jesús es Dios Hijo y nos dirige a la Eucaristía.

2. En la Última Cena, Jesús instituye el Sacramento de la Eucaristía.

3. Jesús les dice a los apóstoles que continúen celebrando la Eucaristía, y sigue siendo así hasta el día de hoy en la Iglesia, en la Santa Misa.

4. La Presencia Real significa que toda la Persona de Jesucristo resucitado está presente en la Eucaristía, en Cuerpo, Alma, Sangre y Divinidad.

5. Cuando el sacerdote pronuncia las palabras de consagración "Éste es Mi Cuerpo" y "Ésta es Mi Sangre", el pan y el vino son transformados en el Cuerpo y en la Sangre de Cristo.

6. La palabra transubstanciación significa que el pan y el vino realmente se convierten en el Cuerpo y en la Sangre de Jesús.

◯ ¡Hablemos Sobre Esto!

1. **¿Cómo nos muestra esta historia que Cristo ofreció el pan y el vino para verdaderamente hacerse Su Cuerpo y Su Sangre?**

2. **Habla sobre cómo podemos realmente unirnos a Jesús en la Última Cena cada vez que asistimos a Misa.**

3. **Platica con tu hijo(a) cómo te sentiste cuando recibiste tu Primera Comunión. ¿Cómo fue para ti un día especial y cómo fue un día que cambió tu vida?**

✝ Leamos la Palabra de Dios
La Última Cena

La lectura de las Sagradas Escrituras para la lección de esta semana fue del Evangelio de San Lucas 22:14–20. Por favor tomen tiempo para leer y reflexionar sobre este pasaje en familia.

Family Fun Activity ✏️

At the Last Supper—a Passover meal—Jesus gave us his Body and Blood to save us from sin and make us strong. At the first Passover, the Israelites ate unleavened bread. The host we receive at Mass is also made of unleavened bread. Many children have never tasted unleavened bread before. Use the simple recipe below to make unleavened bread together while sharing your memories of your own First Holy Communion! This will help your child to know what they can look forward to on their special day when they first receive Jesus in Holy Communion!

🙏 Our Family Prays Together

Parent:

Dear Jesus, we come to your altar to nourish ourselves,

Response:

not with ordinary bread but with yourself, the true bread of eternal life.

Parent:

May the Holy Spirit fill us with his love, and may we prepare ourselves

Response:

to receive your Body and Blood in the Eucharist

Parent:

by getting rid of everything that separates us from you.

Response:

Please prepare my heart to receive you in my First Holy Communion.

All:

Amen.

Unleavened Bread

1 cup whole wheat flour
2 tbsp. extra virgin olive oil
½ cup water

Preheat oven to 350 degrees. Then, in a mixing bowl, combine all ingredients. Put dough onto a floured surface and knead the dough for a few minutes. Roll the dough out until it's about 1/8 inch thick and spread onto a greased cookie sheet or pizza tray. Bake for 20 minutes or until top is light golden. Enjoy!

¡Actividad Familiar ✏ Divertida!

En la Última Cena—una cena de Pascua—Jesús nos dejó Su Cuerpo y Su Sangre para salvarnos del pecado y fortalecernos. En la primera Pascua, los israelitas comieron pan sin levadura. La hostia que recibimos en la Misa también está hecha de pan sin levadura. Muchos niños nunca antes han probado el pan sin levadura.

¡Utiliza la siguiente receta simple para hacer juntos pan sin levadura mientras compartes tus recuerdos de tu propia Primera Comunión! ¡Esto le ayudará a tu hijo(a) a aprender lo que puede esperar de su día especial cuando reciba a Jesús por primera vez en la Santa Comunión!

Receta de pan sin levadura

1 taza de harina de trigo
2 cucharadas de aceite de oliva extra virgen
½ taza de agua

¡Oremos Juntos En Familia!

Papá/Mamá:

Querido Jesús, venimos a Tu altar para alimentarnos,

Respuesta:

no con pan ordinario sino con Tu Cuerpo, el verdadero pan de vida eterna.

Papá/Mamá:

Que el Espíritu Santo nos llene con Su amor y nos prepare

Respuesta:

para recibir Tu Cuerpo y Tu Sangre en la Eucaristía

Papá/Mamá:

al deshacernos de todo lo que nos separe de Ti.

Respuesta:

Te pido que prepares mi corazón para recibirte en mi Primera Comunión.

Todos:

Amén.

Precalienta el horno a 350 grados. Luego mezcla todos los ingredientes en un tazón. Coloca la masa en una superficie con harina y amásala por unos minutos. Usa un rodillo para aplanar la masa hasta que esté aproximadamente 1/8 de pulgada de grosor y acomódala en una charola para hornear o en una charola para pizza. Hornea por 20 minutos o hasta que la superficie esté dorada ligeramente. ¡Disfruta!

♫ Let's Sing God's Praises

Pange Lingua Verses 3 through 6

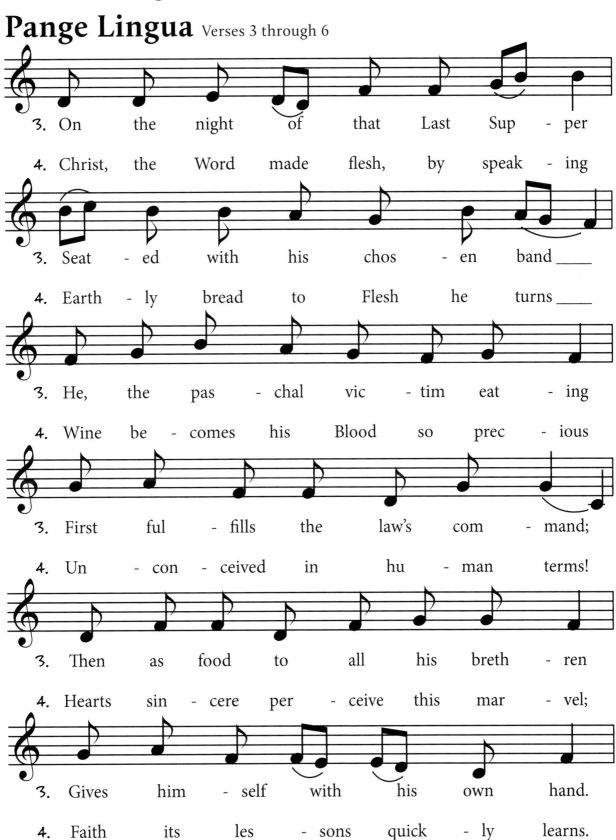

3. On the night of that Last Sup - per

4. Christ, the Word made flesh, by speak - ing

3. Seat - ed with his chos - en band ___

4. Earth - ly bread to Flesh he turns ___

3. He, the pas - chal vic - tim eat - ing

4. Wine be - comes his Blood so prec - ious

3. First ful - fills the law's com - mand;

4. Un - con - ceived in hu - man terms!

3. Then as food to all his breth - ren

4. Hearts sin - cere per - ceive this mar - vel;

3. Gives him - self with his own hand.

4. Faith its les - sons quick - ly learns.

5. Down in ad-or- a- tion fall - ing

6. To the ev- er- last- ing Fath- er

5. This great sac- ra- ment we hail;___

6. And the Son who made us free,___

5. O- ver an- cient forms of wor- ship

6. And the Spir- it, God pro- ceed- ing,

5. New- er rites of grace pre- vail;

6. From them each e- ter- nal- ly,

5. Faith tells us that Christ is pres- ent

6. Be sal- va- tion, hon- or, bless- ing,

5. When our hu- man sens- es fail.

6. Might and end- less maj- es- ty.

Words: Thomas Aquinas (1227–1274)
Sheet Music: Ignatius Press. Used by permission.

Flash Cards

Key Words – Session 2

Mass

Instituted

Memorial

Paschal Mystery

Covenant

Transubstantiation

Flash Cards

Key Words – Session 2 (definitions)

To start or create something that is going to continue.	The Liturgy in which we celebrate the Sacrament of the Eucharist.
Christ's work of redemption, made possible by his Passion (Suffering), Death, Resurrection, and Ascension into Heaven.	A celebration that helps us remember an important past event.
The change of bread and wine into the Body and Blood of Christ.	A sacred relationship with God that makes us part of God's family.

Flash Cards

Key Words – Session 2

✂

Real
Presence

Words of
Consecration

Flash Cards

Key Words – Session 2 (definitions)

The words of Jesus that the priest repeats at Mass—"This is my body," and "This is the chalice of my blood."

The reality that Jesus is truly present, Body, Blood, Soul, and Divinity, in the Eucharist.

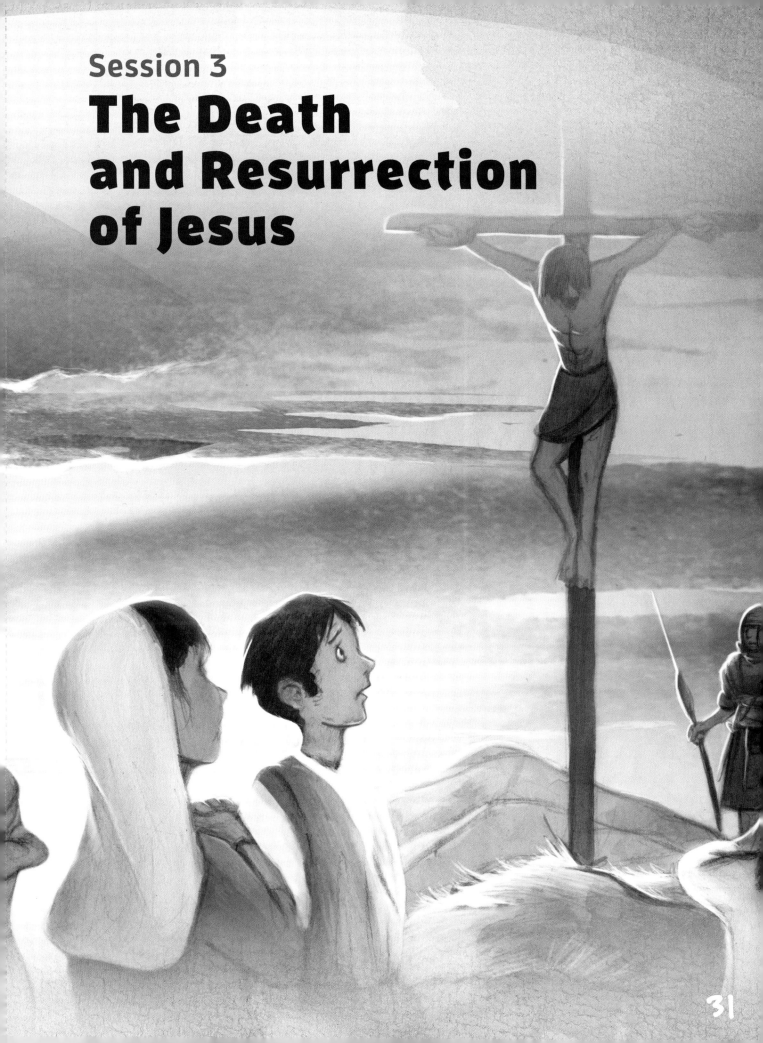

Session 3

The Death and Resurrection of Jesus

☺ Connect — Opening Activity

Jesus Opened the Gates of Heaven

Jesus died on the Cross for our salvation. He saved us from our sins and opened the gates of Heaven so we can live with God in Heaven someday!

Place the stickers, to see Jesus opening the gates and welcoming us!

Let's Live It
Jesus Saves Us!

Jesus's Death and Resurrection saves us and calls us to live in a way that leads others to him!

Unscramble the words below to answer each clue.

1. When Jesus died on the Cross to free us from sin.

   xnficucioir _ _ _ _ _ _ _ _ _ _ _

2. Jesus rose from the dead overcoming the power of death.

   isruetrocern _ _ _ _ _ _ _ _ _ _ _ _

3. Forty days after his Resurrection, Jesus went to Heaven.

   naoncsise _ _ _ _ _ _ _ _ _

4. Fifty days after his Resurrection, Jesus sent the Holy Spirit to guide the Church.

   tcnepseto _ _ _ _ _ _ _ _ _

5. We are called to be this. Jesus wants us to show his love to the world and lead others to him.

   swsetensi _ _ _ _ _ _ _ _ _

6. Jesus's Body, Blood, Soul, and Divinity. He gives us the gift of his very life in our souls every time we receive it.

   iahcesrut _ _ _ _ _ _ _ _ _

WORD BANK

Ascension   **Eucharist**   **Witnesses**

Crucifixion   **Resurrection**   **Pentecost**

Jesus Said,

"But you shall receive power when the Holy Spirit has come upon you; and you shall be my witnesses..."

—Acts 1:8

The Greatest Gift

When you go to Mass every Sunday, you will be able to receive this awesome gift of Holy Communion! Draw a picture below of your family sitting in the pew at Mass. Then write on the lines below how it makes you feel that Jesus wants to give you the gift of himself.

_____

_____

> *"For as often as you eat this bread and drink the chalice, you proclaim the Lord's death until he comes."*
>
> —1 Corinthians 11:26

☑ Things We Learned This Week

1. Jesus is the new Passover Lamb who sacrificed himself to save us from sin.

2. With Jesus's Death, Resurrection, and Ascension into Heaven, the gates of Heaven were opened for the salvation of all God's children.

3. Sanctifying Grace is God's life in our souls. Actual grace is the help God gives us to make correct choices.

4. Pentecost was when the Holy Spirit came down on Mary and the Apostles and gave them strength to be witnesses for Christ.

5. We are the Body of Christ and continue the mission of Jesus to be witnesses of his love wherever we go.

💬 Let's Talk About It

1. **Jesus gave his life freely on the Cross for all of us. How does this show his love for us?**

2. **Talk about why it is important that we show our love for Jesus by going to Mass every Sunday.**

3. **Discuss with your child ways that we can bring Christ's love into your home.**

✝ Let's Read God's Word

The Scripture reading for this week was John 19:28–20:10. Please take the time to read and reflect on this passage as a family.

☑ Lo que aprendimos esta semana:

1. La resurrección se refiere a Jesús que resucita de entre los muertos al tercer día después de Su muerte en la Cruz.

2. La muerte, resurrección y ascensión de Jesús al cielo abrió las puertas del cielo para la salvación de todos los hijos de Dios.

3. La gracia es la vida de Jesús en nuestras almas. La gracia actual es el don de Dios para ayudarnos en cada momento a amar a Dios y tomar las decisiones correctas. La gracia santificante es el don de la propia vida divina de Dios en nosotros y que nos santifica.

4. Pentecostés es cuando el Espíritu Santo descendió sobre María y los apóstoles, cincuenta días después de Su resurrección, diez días después de que Jesús ascendió al cielo. Pentecostés es el nacimiento de la Iglesia.

5. Somos el Cuerpo de Cristo y continuamos la misión de Jesús siendo testigos de Su amor a donde quiera que vayamos. La Eucaristía nos fortalece para esta misión.

○ ¡Hablemos Sobre Esto!

1. Jesús dio libremente Su vida en la cruz por todos nosotros. ¿Cómo muestra este acto Su amor hacia nosotros? ¿Alguna vez sacrificaste algo que era importante para ti por ayudar a alguien más?

2. ¿Por qué es importante que mostremos nuestro amor por Jesús al asistir a Misa cada domingo? Platiquen sobre esto.

3. Platica con tu hijo(a) algunas maneras en que podemos llevar el amor de Cristo a nuestro hogar y a donde quiera que vayamos.

Leamos la Palabra de Dios

La lectura de las Sagradas Escrituras para la lección de esta semana fue del Evangelio de San Juan 19:28–20:10. Por favor tomen tiempo para leer y reflexionar sobre este pasaje en familia.

Family Fun Activity ✏️

This week we have been talking about honoring the Lord's Day by going to Mass each Sunday. To help your children understand the readings at Mass better, your family can watch *Opening the Word* each week for a wonderful 5- to 7-minute reflection on the Sunday readings. This is a free offering on the homepage of the website: formed.org.

Explore the Faith Together

For more information on Catholic traditions and teachings as well as Catholic movies, books, audios, and more, please check out formed.org. Ask your Director of Religious Education if your parish has a subscription to log on for free!

🙏 Our Family Prays Together

Act of Faith

Parent:

O my God, I firmly believe that you are one God in three divine Persons,

Response:

Father, Son, and Holy Spirit;

Parent:

I believe that your divine Son became man and died for our sins,

Response:

and that he shall come to judge the living and the dead.

Parent:

I believe these and all the truths that the holy Catholic Church teaches,

Response:

because you have revealed them, who can neither deceive nor be deceived.

All:

Amen.

¡Actividad Familiar ✏ Divertida!

Esta semana hemos estado hablando de santificar el Día del Señor asistiendo a Misa cada domingo. Para ayudarle a tu hijo(a) a entender mejor las lecturas de la Misa, tu familia puede ver el programa *Opening the Word* cada semana, para reflexionar con un video de 5 a 7 minutos las lecturas dominicales. Este programa es gratuito en la página del sitio de internet: formed.org.

Exploren Juntos La Fe

Para más información acerca de las tradiciones y enseñanzas católicas, y para encontrar material católico como películas, libros, audios, etc., puedes checar la página formed. org. ¡Pregúntale al director de educación religiosa si tu parroquia tiene una suscripción parroquial para tener acceso gratuito!

✋ ¡Oremos Juntos En Familia!

Acto de Fe

Papá/Mamá:

Oh mi Dios, firmemente creo que eres un solo Dios en tres Personas divinas,

Respuesta:

Padre, Hijo y Espíritu Santo;

Papá/Mamá:

Creo que Tu divino Hijo se hizo hombre y murió por nuestros pecados,

Respuesta:

y que vendrá a juzgar a vivos y a muertos.

Papá/Mamá:

Creo estas y todas las verdades que enseña la santa Iglesia Católica,

Respuesta:

porque nos las has revelado, Tú, que no engañas ni puedes ser engañado.

Todos:

Amén.

♫ Let's Sing God's Praises

Pange Lingua Verses 3 through 6

3. On the night of that Last Sup - per

4. Christ, the Word made flesh, by speak - ing

3. Seat - ed with his chos - en band ____

4. Earth - ly bread to Flesh he turns ____

3. He, the pas - chal vic - tim eat - ing

4. Wine be - comes his Blood so prec - ious

3. First ful - fills the law's com - mand;

4. Un - con - ceived in hu - man terms!

3. Then as food to all his breth - ren

4. Hearts sin - cere per - ceive this mar - vel;

3. Gives him - self with his own hand.

4. Faith its les - sons quick - ly learns.

5. Down in ad- or- a- tion fall - ing
6. To the ev- er- last- ing Fath- er

5. This great sac- ra- ment we hail;____
6. And the Son who made us free,____

5. O- ver an- cient forms of wor- ship
6. And the Spir- it, God pro- ceed- ing,

5. New- er rites of grace pre- vail;
6. From them each e- ter- nal- ly,

5. Faith tells us that Christ is pres- ent
6. Be sal- va- tion, hon- or, bless- ing,

5. When our hu- man sens- es fail.
6. Might and end- less maj- es- ty.

Words: Thomas Aquinas (1227–1274)
Sheet Music: Ignatius Press. Used by permission.

Flash Cards

Key Words – Session 3

Crucified

Sabbath

Salvation

Resurrection

Ascension

Pentecost

Flash Cards

Key Words – Session 3 (definitions)

The seventh day of the week, or Saturday.

To put to death by nailing or tying a person to a cross as a form of punishment.

Jesus's rising from the dead on the third day after his Death on the Cross.

The forgiveness of our sins and healing of our friendship with God so that we can be with him in Heaven.

The descent of the Holy Spirit upon Mary and the Apostles.

When Jesus went up into Heaven, forty days after his Resurrection.

Flash Cards

Key Words – Session 3

Body of Christ

Witnesses

Chrism

Sanctifying Grace

Actual Grace

Flash Cards

Key Words – Session 3 (definitions)

People who tell others the truth about what they have seen and heard.

Another name for the Catholic Church.

The gift of God's own divine life in us that makes us holy.

The blessed oil used for anointing in Baptism and Confirmation.

God's gift to help us in each moment to love God and make the right choices.

ATTENTION PARENTS!

Dear Parents,

Over the past few weeks, we have been talking about how the Lord has prepared his people for his great sacrifice on the Cross and the mystery of the Eucharist. In the Old Testament, God asked the Israelites to make a Tabernacle tent to hold his  very presence. Today, in every Catholic church, we have a Tabernacle where the consecrated Hosts—the Real Presence of Christ in the Eucharist—is kept for prayer and adoration.

Next week your child will be making a little "tabernacle" to keep all of his or her special holy items and First Communion gifts. We are asking each family to send a small box for the next class (preferably the size of a shoe box). If you have any additional boxes, please send those as well, just in case some children forget theirs.

Thanks so much for your participation in this special project and in all the ways you are preparing your child to receive and treasure the Eucharist!

Many Blessings!

¡ATENCIÓN PADRES DE FAMILIA!

Estimados padres de familia:,

En las semanas anteriores, hemos estado hablando de cómo el Señor ha preparado a Su pueblo para comprender Su gran sacrificio en la cruz y el misterio de la Eucaristía.

En el Antiguo Testamento, Dios les pidió a los israelitas que hicieran una tienda de Tabernáculo donde tendrían Su presencia.

Hoy, en cada iglesia Católica, tenemos un Tabernáculo donde se guardan las Hostias consagradas—la Presencia Real de Cristo en la Eucaristía.

La próxima semana su hijo estará trabajando en construir un pequeño "tabernáculo", donde podrá guardar todos sus artículos religiosos y sus regalos de Primera Comunión. Le pedimos a cada familia que envíen una caja pequeña para la siguiente clase (de preferencia del tamaño de una caja de zapatos). Si tuvieran algunas cajas adicionales para donar, por favor envíenlas también, en caso de que algún niño olvide la suya.

¡Les agradecemos por su participación en este proyecto especial y en todas las formas en que ustedes están preparando a su hijo para recibir y atesorar la Eucaristía!

¡Les deseamos muchas bendiciones!

Session 4
The Sacrament of the Eucharist

☺ Connect — Opening Activity

Jesus Is the Bread of Life!

Jesus fed more than 5,000 people with just a few loaves of bread and two fish. Today he does an even more amazing miracle! He feeds us in the Eucharist with his own Body and Blood! Place the stickers and color the picture.

Let's Live It
The Sacrament of the Eucharist

The Sacrament of the Eucharist is so important that the Church has many different names for it. Each name teaches us something different about the sacrament.

Use the words in the word bank to fill in the blanks below.

1. _____ means "thanksgiving" in Greek. We give thanks to God for this sacrament.

2. We often call this sacrament Jesus's _____ ____ _____, but it is actually his Body, Blood, Soul, and Divinity.

3. Jesus called this sacrament the _____ ___ _____ because it is true food to give life to our souls.

4. You will receive your First Holy _____ soon. It means that you will have a special union with Jesus.

5. The consecrated _____ is the precious Body of Jesus.

6. The _____ _____ _____ is another name for the Eucharist because it is the center of the sacramental life of the Church.

7. This sacrament is called the _____ _____ of the Mass because it makes Jesus's sacrifice on the Cross present to us.

8. Jesus gave us his Body and Blood at the Last Supper, so we call this sacrament the _____ _____.

WORD BANK

Communion

Lord's Supper

Holy Sacrifice

Eucharist

Most Blessed Sacrament

Bread of Life

Host

Body and Blood

Jesus Said,

"As the living Father sent me, and I live because of the Father, so he who eats me will live because of me."
—John 6:57

We Are Thankful for the Eucharist!

The Eucharist is the greatest gift that Jesus gives to us—it is his very life in our souls! Eucharist means "thanksgiving" in Greek; we are thankful for Jesus's gift of himself to us.

Write a short thank you letter to Jesus to tell him how thankful you are for all the gifts he has given you!

Dear Jesus,

_____

_____

_____

_____

_____

_____

_____

_____

_____

Sincerely,

_____

"Rejoice always, pray constantly, give thanks in all circumstances; for this is the will of God in Christ Jesus for you."
—1 Thessalonians 5:18

☑ Things We Learned This Week

1. The Real Presence is the teaching that Jesus is really and fully present, Body, Blood, Soul, and Divinity, in the Eucharist. Because of this, the Eucharist is the source and summit of our Catholic Faith.

2. Jesus unites himself with us and gives us grace when we receive the Sacrament of the Eucharist.

3. Jesus says that his Body is true food and his Blood is true drink that will give our souls eternal life. He is the true Bread from Heaven.

4. Every tiny piece of the Host and every drop of the Precious Blood is Jesus—Body, Blood, Soul, and Divinity. The Eucharist that we receive is the risen Body and Blood of Christ.

5. The Eucharist is so important in our Faith that we call it by many names, such as, Eucharist—which means thanksgiving—Holy Communion, and Holy Sacrifice.

☐ Let's Talk About It

1. Jesus knew that just as our bodies need good food to keep us strong and healthy, so too our souls need the Eucharist to be strong. Can you name one or two ways that having a strong soul can help you?

2. Talk about how Jesus's Real Presence in the Eucharist shows how close he wants to be with us.

3. Discuss with your child some ways that being close to Jesus has helped you.

✝ Let's Read God's Word
Jesus Is the Bread of Life

The Scripture reading for this week's lesson was from John 6:1–59. Please take time to read and reflect on this passage as a family.

☑ Lo que aprendimos esta semana:

◯ ¡Hablemos Sobre Esto!

1. La Presencia Real es la enseñanza de que Jesús está real y completamente presente en Cuerpo, Alma y Divinidad, en la Eucaristía. Por eso, la Eucaristía es la fuente y culmen de nuestra fe católica.

2. Jesús nos une a sí mismo y nos otorga la gracia cuando recibimos el Sacramento de la Eucaristía.

3. Jesús dijo que Su Cuerpo es verdadera comida y Su Sangre es verdadera bebida que dará a nuestras almas vida eterna. Él es el verdadero pan del cielo.

4. Cada pedacito de la Hostia y cada gota de la preciosísima Sangre es el mismo Jesús, en Cuerpo, Sangre, Alma y Divinidad. La Eucaristía que recibimos es el Cuerpo y la Sangre de Cristo resucitado.

5. La Eucaristía es tan importante en nuestra fe que le llamamos por distintos nombres, tales como: Eucaristía, que significa acción de gracias, Sagrada Comunión y Santo Sacrificio.

1. Jesús sabía que así como nuestros cuerpos necesitan de buen alimento para mantenernos fuertes y saludables, así también nuestras almas necesitan la Eucaristía para ser fuertes. ¿Puedes nombrar una o dos maneras en que te puede ayudar el que tengas un alma fuerte?

2. Platiquen sobre cómo la presencia real de Jesús en la Eucaristía nos muestra qué tan cerca desea estar Jesús de nosotros.

3. Platica con tu hijo(a) algunas maneras en que te ha ayudado estar cerca de Jesús.

✝ Leamos la Palabra de Dios
Jesús es el Pan de Vida

La lectura de las Sagradas Escrituras para la lección de esta semana fue del Evangelio de San Juan 6:1–51. Por favor tomen tiempo para leer y reflexionar sobre este pasaje en familia.

Family Fun Activity

Visit the Blessed Sacrament at your parish as a family. This would be a wonderful time to show your child the Adoration Chapel if your church has one. Or you could go into the main sanctuary and show your child the Tabernacle where the Eucharist is kept. Feel free to bring this sheet and pray the Act of Spiritual Communion at this special time.

Explore the Faith Together

For more information on Catholic traditions and teachings as well as Catholic movies, books, audios, and more, please check out formed.org. Ask your Director of Religious Education if your parish has a subscription to log on for free!

Our Family Prays Together

Act of Spiritual Communion

Parent:

My Jesus, I believe that you are present in the Most Holy Sacrament.

Response:

I love you above all things, and I desire to receive you into my soul.

Parent:

Since I cannot at this moment receive you sacramentally, come at least spiritually into my heart.

Response:

I embrace you as if you were already there and unite myself to you.

Parent:

Never permit me to be separated from you.

Response:

Prepare my heart to receive my First Holy Communion.

All:

Amen.

¡Actividad Familiar Divertida!

Visita el Santísimo Sacramento en tu parroquia como familia. Si tu parroquia tiene una capilla de adoración sería un buen momento para mostrársela a tu hijo(a). O puedes ir al santuario principal y mostrarle a tu hijo(a) el Tabernáculo donde se guarda la Eucaristía. Puedes llevarte esta hoja y hacer la oración del Acto de comunión espiritual en este tiempo especial.

Exploren Juntos La Fe

Para más información acerca de las tradiciones y enseñanzas católicas, y para encontrar material católico como películas, libros, audios, etc., puedes checar la página formed. org. ¡Pregúntale al director de educación religiosa si tu parroquia tiene una suscripción parroquial para tener acceso gratuito!

¡Oremos Juntos En Familia!

Acto de comunión espiritual

Papá/Mamá:

Mi Jesús, creo que estás presente en el Santísimo Sacramento.

Respuesta:

Te amo sobre todas las cosas y deseo recibirte en mi alma.

Papá/Mamá:

Mas ya que no puedo recibirte en este momento sacramentalmente, ven por lo menos espiritualmente a mi corazón.

Respuesta:

Yo me abrazo todo a Ti.

Papá/Mamá:

No permitas que nada ni nadie me aparte de Ti.

Respuesta:

Prepara mi corazón para recibir mi Primera Comunión.

Todos:

Amén.

♪ Let's Sing God's Praises

Pange Lingua Verses 3 through 6

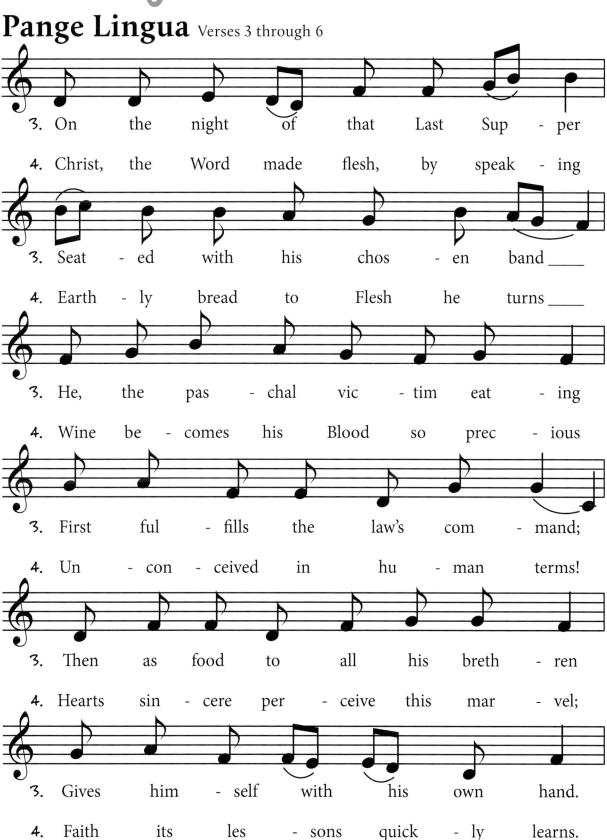

3. On the night of that Last Sup - per

4. Christ, the Word made flesh, by speak - ing

3. Seat - ed with his chos - en band ___

4. Earth - ly bread to Flesh he turns ___

3. He, the pas - chal vic - tim eat - ing

4. Wine be - comes his Blood so prec - ious

3. First ful - fills the law's com - mand;

4. Un - con - ceived in hu - man terms!

3. Then as food to all his breth - ren

4. Hearts sin - cere per - ceive this mar - vel;

3. Gives him - self with his own hand.

4. Faith its les - sons quick - ly learns.

5. Down in ad- or- a- tion fall - ing

6. To the ev- er- last- ing Fath- er

5. This great sac- ra- ment we hail;____

6. And the Son who made us free,____

5. O- ver an- cient forms of wor- ship

6. And the Spir- it, God pro- ceed- ing,

5. New- er rites of grace pre- vail;

6. From them each e- ter- nal- ly,

5. Faith tells us that Christ is pres- ent

6. Be sal- va- tion, hon- or, bless- ing,

5. When our hu- man sens- es fail.

6. Might and end- less maj- es- ty.

Words: Thomas Aquinas (1227–1274)
Sheet Music: Ignatius Press. Used by permission.

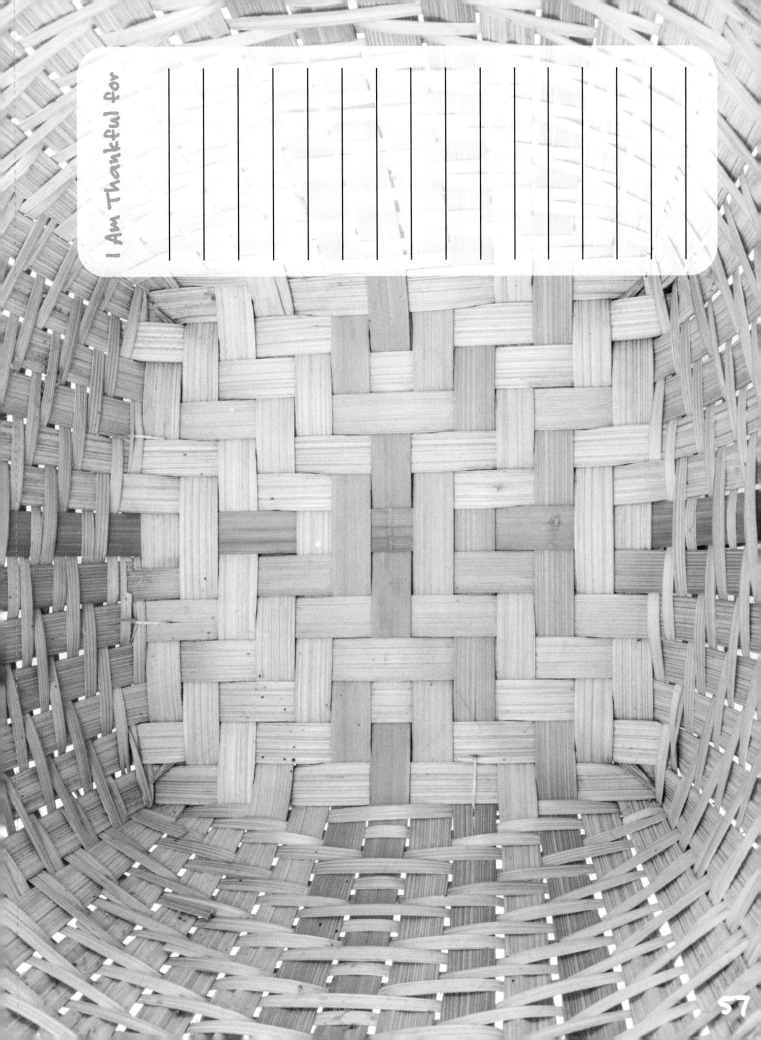

I Am Thankful for

57

Session 1
Preparing the Way for Christ

Session 2
The Last Supper

Session 3
The Death and Resurrection of Jesus

Session 4
The Sacrament of the Eucharist

Session 5
Receiving Holy Communion

NO FALSE GODS

Session 6
The Liturgy of the Mass

Session 7
The Liturgy of the Word

Session 8
The Liturgy of the Eucharist

Flash Cards

Key Words – Session 4

Miracle

Heaven

Bread of Life Discourse

Host

Tabernacle

Genuflect

Flash Cards

Key Words – Session 4 (definitions)

The place where God dwells along with the angels and the saints.

A sign or wonder that can only be worked by God.

The small wafer or piece of unleavened bread that becomes the Body of Christ.

Jesus's teaching on the Eucharist in the Gospel of John, chapter 6.

To bend the right knee to the floor or ground to show love and respect to Christ in the Tabernacle.

An ornate, box-like container where the Eucharist is kept for the purpose of Adoration outside of Mass.

Flash Cards

Key Words – Session 4

Venial Sins

Act of Spiritual Communion

Eucharist

Lord's Supper

Holy Sacrifice

The Most Blessed Sacrament

Key Words – Session 4 (definitions)

A prayer in which we tell Jesus how much we want to be united with him.

Lesser sins that do not result in a complete separation from God.

The Passover meal that Jesus shared with his Apostles on the night of his Crucifixion.

The sacrament instituted by Christ at the Last Supper, in which bread and wine are changed into his Body and Blood.

Another name for the Eucharist because it is the center of the sacramental life of the Church.

In the Liturgy of the Mass, the sacrifice of Jesus on the Cross is made present to us.

Flash Cards

Key Words – Session 4

Holy Communion

Flash Cards

Key Words – Session 4 (definitions)

Another name for the Sacrament of the Eucharist because it unites us with Jesus.

Receiving Holy Communion

☺ Connect — Opening Activity

Saint Paul Writes about the Eucharist

Saint Paul spread the Good News of Jesus all over the world. He wrote letters to the Christians he visited. These letters were so special they became part of the Bible.

Color the picture below and place the stickers in Saint Paul's thought bubbles.

Let's Live It
Preparing to Receive

Receiving Jesus in the Eucharist is the most important and special thing we can do as Catholics! Read the statements below about preparing to receive Holy Communion.

Put a "T" by the true statements and an "F" by the false statements.

1. _____ The Eucharist fills our souls with grace so we can love God and others more.

2. _____ If I have committed a mortal sin, I need to go to Confession before I receive the Eucharist.

3. _____ We don't need to go to Mass every Sunday, especially if we have important things to do.

4. _____ I should fast from food and drink for one hour before Communion, except for water or medicine.

5. _____ I should only receive Communion in the hand, never on the tongue.

6. _____ Jesus is fully present—Body, Blood, Soul, and Divinity—in every drop of the Precious Blood and in every piece of the Host.

7. _____ All of my venial sins are washed away when I receive Holy Communion.

8. _____ The Eucharist unites us with Jesus but not really with the Church.

Jesus Said,
"For my flesh is food indeed, and my blood is drink indeed."
—John 6:55

Dear Jesus

We learned this week that we can go to Adoration to worship Jesus in the Blessed Sacrament. Adoration is a very special time when we can talk to Jesus in the presence of the Blessed Sacrament. Many Catholic churches have Adoration Chapels where the Blessed Sacrament is kept.

On the lines below, write a special prayer to Jesus that you can bring to Adoration. Then draw a picture of a Monstrance or the Tabernacle in your church.

_____

_____

_____

Jesus Said,

"He who eats my flesh and drinks my blood has eternal life, and I will raise him up at the last day."

—John 6:54

☑ Things We Learned This Week

1. Jesus is truly present in the Eucharist—Body, Blood, Soul, and Divinity—in every drop of the Precious Blood and in every piece of the Host.

2. Receiving the Eucharist at Mass is so important that we should do some special things to prepare our bodies and our souls.

3. We prepare our bodies to hunger for Jesus by fasting from food and drink for one hour before receiving Holy Communion. We prepare our souls by going to Confession if we have committed a mortal sin so we can receive Jesus in the state of grace.

4. We can receive the Host on the tongue or in the hand, where we have made our hands like a throne for Jesus.

5. We receive special graces when we receive the Eucharist: we have a very special union with Christ and with his Church, our baptismal graces are increased and renewed, our venial sins are washed away, and we grow in love of God and of others.

💬 Let's Talk About It

1. Jesus wants to be so close to us that he comes to live in our hearts and in our souls. How can we grow closer to the people that we love? How can we grow closer to Jesus?

2. Talk about how you prefer to receive Holy Communion—on the tongue or in the hand—and why. Then have your child practice receiving both ways to discern what is most comfortable for him or her.

3. Discuss with your child some ways to prepare for receiving Holy Communion for the first time.

✝ Let's Read God's Word
Saint Paul Writes about the Eucharist

The Scripture reading for this week's lesson was from 1 Corinthians 10:14–17. Please take time to read and reflect on this passage as a family.

☑ Lo que aprendimos esta semana:

1. Jesús está verdaderamente presente en la Eucaristía, en Cuerpo, Sangre, Alma y Divinidad, en cada gota de la preciosísima Sangre y en cada pedacito de la Hostia.

2. Es tan importante recibir al Eucaristía en la Misa, que deberíamos hacer algo especial para preparar nuestros cuerpos y nuestras almas.

3. Preparamos nuestros cuerpos para tener hambre de Jesús ayunando de comida y bebida por una hora antes de recibir la Sagrada Comunión. Preparamos nuestras almas yendo a confesarnos si hemos cometido algún pecado mortal, para poder recibir a Jesús en estado de gracia.

4. Recibimos gracias especiales cuando recibimos la Eucaristía: tenemos una unión muy especial con Cristo y Su Iglesia, nuestra gracia bautismal se incrementa y renueva, nuestros pecados veniales son perdonados y crecemos en amor a Dios y al prójimo.

◯ ¡Hablemos Sobre Esto!

1. Jesús desea estar tan cerca de nosotros, que Él viene a habitar en nuestros corazones y en nuestras almas. ¿Cómo podemos acercarnos más a las personas que amamos? ¿Cómo podemos acercarnos más a Jesús?

2. Platiquen sobre cómo prefieren recibir la Sagrada Comunión, si en la lengua o en las manos, y por qué. Luego haz que tu hijo(a) practique recibiendo de ambas formas la Eucaristía, para discernir cuál es la que prefiere.

3. Platica con tu hijo(a) algunas maneras de cómo prepararse para recibir la Sagrada Comunión por primera vez.

Leamos la Palabra de Dios
San Pablo escribe sobre la Eucaristía

La lectura de las Sagradas Escrituras para la lección de esta semana fue de la 1ª Carta de San Pablo a los Corintios 10:14–17. Por favor tomen tiempo para leer y reflexionar sobre este pasaje en familia.

Family Fun Activity

This week take a few minutes after Mass to adore the Eucharist together as a family. If your parish has an Adoration Chapel, this would be the perfect place. You can show your child the Tabernacle where the consecrated Host is kept and spend a few minutes in quiet prayer. If your parish does not have a special Adoration Chapel, you can just kneel in a pew after Mass and pray quietly for a few minutes together. Allow this time with Jesus to bring you closer to him and to each other. These are just some of the graces we receive from the Eucharist!

Our Family Prays Together

A Prayer Before Communion

Parent:

O Lord Jesus Christ,

Response:

Son of the living God,

Parent:

by your Death and Resurrection,

Response:

you have given life to the world

Parent:

may your Body and Blood,

Response:

which I am about to receive in Holy Communion,

Parent:

keep me from sin and from every evil.

Response:

Help me to follow your commandments always

Parent:

and never let me be separated from you.

All:

Amen.

¡Actividad Familiar Divertida!

Esta semana toma unos minutos después de Misa para adorar la Eucaristía juntos en familia. El lugar perfecto sería en la capilla de adoración, si tu parroquia tiene una. Le puedes mostrar a tu hijo(a) el Tabernáculo, donde se guardan las Hostias consagradas, y pasar ahí unos minutos en oración en silencio. Si tu parroquia no tiene una capilla de adoración especial, pueden tan solo hincarse en una de las bancas después de Misa y orar en silencio por unos minutos todos juntos. Permitan que este tiempo con Jesús los acerque más a Él y entre ustedes. ¡Éstas son solamente algunas de las gracias que recibimos en la Eucaristía!

¡Oremos Juntos En Familia!

Oración para antes de la Comunión

Papá/Mamá:

Oh Señor Jesucristo,

Respuesta:

Hijo del Dios vivo,

Papá/Mamá:

que, por Tu muerte y resurrección,

Respuesta:

has dado vida al mundo,

Papá/Mamá:

que así también por Tu Cuerpo y Sangre

Respuesta:

que voy a recibir en la Sagrada Comunión,

Papá/Mamá:

me libres de todos mis pecados y de cualquier peligro.

Respuesta:

Ayúdame a siempre seguir Tus mandamientos,

Papá/Mamá:

y a nunca separarme de Ti.

Todos:

Amén.

♫ Let's Sing God's Praises

Pange Lingua Verses 3 through 6

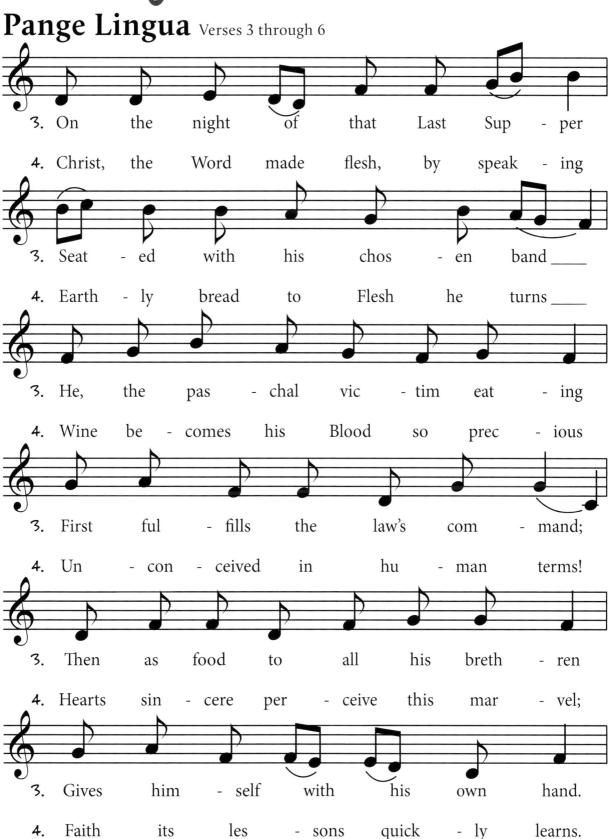

3. On the night of that Last Sup - per

4. Christ, the Word made flesh, by speak - ing

3. Seat - ed with his chos - en band ____

4. Earth - ly bread to Flesh he turns ____

3. He, the pas - chal vic - tim eat - ing

4. Wine be - comes his Blood so prec - ious

3. First ful - fills the law's com - mand;

4. Un - con - ceived in hu - man terms!

3. Then as food to all his breth - ren

4. Hearts sin - cere per - ceive this mar - vel;

3. Gives him - self with his own hand.

4. Faith its les - sons quick - ly learns.

73

5. Down in ad- or- a- tion fall - ing

6. To the ev- er- last- ing Fath- er

5. This great sac- ra- ment we hail;____

6. And the Son who made us free,____

5. O- ver an- cient forms of wor- ship

6. And the Spir- it, God pro- ceed- ing,

5. New- er rites of grace pre- vail;

6. From them each e- ter- nal- ly,

5. Faith tells us that Christ is pres- ent

6. Be sal- va- tion, hon- or, bless- ing,

5. When our hu- man sens- es fail.

6. Might and end- less maj- es- ty.

Words: Thomas Aquinas (1227–1274)
Sheet Music: Ignatius Press. Used by permission.

Flash Cards

Key Words – Session 5

State of Grace

Mortal Sin

Reverence

Eucharistic Fast

Consecrated

Monstrance

Flash Cards

Key Words – Session 5 (definitions)

A serious sin that separates us from God.	The state of having God's divine life of grace within us.
The rule that we must not eat or drink anything for at least one hour before receiving Holy Communion.	To show respect, especially for things that are holy.
The special vessel that is used to display the Blessed Sacrament for Adoration.	The bread and wine that has been changed into the Body and Blood of Jesus.

Flash Cards

Key Words – Session 5

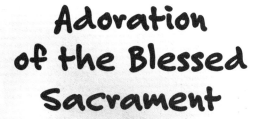

Adoration
of the Blessed
Sacrament

Flash Cards

Key Words – Session 5 (definitions)

The special act of worshipping Jesus present in the Blessed Sacrament.

The Liturgy of the Mass

☺ Connect — Opening Activity

The Mass Makes Christ Present

Every time we go to Mass, we recall special events in the life of Jesus, and his sacrifice on the Cross is made present.

Put the correct sticker in each box, then draw yourself in the last box showing that at Mass you are truly united to Christ who is made present.

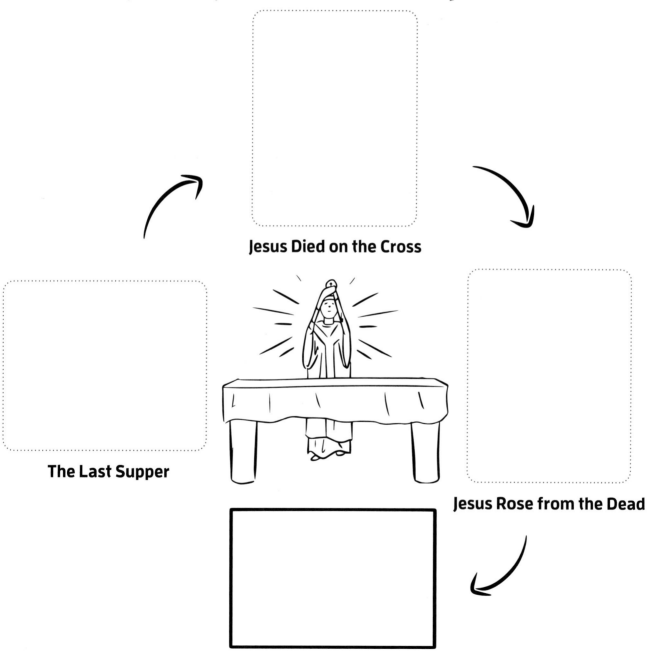

Jesus Died on the Cross

The Last Supper

Jesus Rose from the Dead

Jesus Becomes Present with You at Every Mass

80

© 2018 Augustine Institute

Let's Live It

The Liturgy of the Mass

At Mass, we really participate in God's saving work! Fill in the missing words below. Then use the circled letters to discover another name for the Holy Mass— and our worship of God both on earth and in Heaven.

1. We go to Mass on Sunday because it is the ○_ _ _'_ _ _ _ , the day of Jesus's Resurrection.

2. At every Mass, Jesus's _ _ _ _○_ _ _ _ on the Cross is made present to us.

3. The Liturgy of the Mass crosses space and time to allow us to _ _ _○_ _ _ _ _ _ _ in Jesus's sacrifice.

4. The _ _ _ _ _○_ _ _ _ was when Christ instituted the Mass.

5. Jesus gave us the Mass when he said, "Do this in ○_ _ _ _ _ _ _ _ _ _ of me."

6. Because Jesus gave us this great gift, we have an _ _ _ _○_ _ _ _ _ to go to Mass every Sunday.

7. The Mass recalls the important events of salvation _ _ _ _ _ _○.

At Mass we worship with the angels and saints in the heavenly

_ _ _ _ _ _ _ .

WORD BANK

obligation   sacrifice   Lord's Day   Last Supper

participate   history   remembrance

Keep Holy the Lord's Day!

We learned this week that we should make Sundays very special because it is the Lord's Day. It is the day that Jesus rose from the dead, and that is why we go to Mass on Sundays. In addition to going to Mass, what is one other way that you can make the Lord's Day special? Write your idea on the lines below, and draw a picture.

_____

_____

_____

The Third Commandment
"Remember the sabbath day, to keep it holy."

—Exodus 20:8

☑ Things We Learned This Week

1. The Liturgy of the Mass is our public worship and participation in the work of God.

2. The sacrifice of Jesus on the Cross is made present at Mass.

3. The Mass is celebrated on Sunday because that is the day the Lord was raised from the dead. As Christians, we have the gift and obligation to attend Mass every Sunday and on Holy Days of Obligation.

4. At Mass, we participate in the one sacrifice of Jesus on the Cross, and in Holy Communion we receive the Body and Blood of Christ.

5. Each Mass is a participation in the heavenly liturgy, where we worship God with all the angels and saints in Heaven.

◯ Let's Talk About It

1. When Jesus gave us the Mass, he told us to "do this in remembrance of me." Why do you think that Jesus gave us the great gift of the Mass? How does it help us to live a Christian life?

2. Talk about one thing your family can do each Sunday to prepare better for going to Mass.

3. Discuss with your son or daughter how our participation at Mass gives us grace and helps the Scripture become real to us. What are some ways that you can participate fully at Mass?

✝ Let's Read God's Word

The Letter of Saint Paul to the Corinthians

The Scripture reading for this week's lesson was from 1 Corinthians 11:23–29. Please take time to read and reflect on this passage as a family.

☑ Lo que aprendimos esta semana:

1. La liturgia de la Misa es nuestra adoración pública y nuestra participación en la obra de Dios.

2. La Última Cena, la crucifixión, la resurrección y la ascensión de Jesús al cielo son eventos que se hacen presentes en la Santa Misa.

3. La Misa se celebra los domingos porque es el día en que el Señor resucitó de entre los muertos. Como cristianos, tenemos el don y la obligación de asistir a Misa cada domingo y los días de guardar.

4. En la Misa, participamos en el único sacrifico de Jesús en la cruz, y en la Sagrada Comunión recibimos el Cuerpo y la Sangre de Cristo.

5. Cada Misa es una participación en la liturgia celestial, donde adoramos a Dios con todos los ángeles y santos en el cielo.

💬 ¡Hablemos Sobre Esto!

1. Cuando Jesús nos dio la Misa, nos dijo que hiciéramos esto en memoria suya. ¿Por qué crees que Jesús nos dio el gran regalo de la Misa? ¿Cómo nos ayuda a vivir una vida cristiana?

2. Platiquen sobre una cosa que su familia puede hacer cada domingo para prepararse mejor para ir a Misa.

3. Habla con tu hijo(a) sobre cómo nuestra participación en la Misa nos otorga gracia y nos ayuda a que las Escrituras sean más reales para nosotros. ¿Cuáles son algunas formas en que puedes participar plenamente en la Misa?

Leamos la Palabra de Dios

La Carta de San Pablo a los Corintios

La lectura de las Sagradas Escrituras para la lección de esta semana fue de la 1ª Carta de San Pablo a los Corintios 11:23–26. Por favor tomen tiempo para leer y reflexionar sobre este pasaje en familia.

Family Fun Activity ✏️

This week sit down together to decorate a journal or notebook for each member of the family to take to Mass each week. Encourage each family member to use this during the Mass to note any special thoughts or reflections on the readings or homily. Children can draw the scenes being described in the Scripture stories so that they become more real to them, or they can write a little prayer to Jesus in the quiet time before or after Communion.

🤚 Our Family Prays Together

A Prayer After Communion

Parent:

I believe, O Lord, that you are the Son of the living God.

Response:

I believe that you came into the world to save sinners, and I believe that the Eucharist is your Body and Blood.

Parent:

Therefore, I pray, have mercy on me and forgive me for sins I have committed,

Response:

in my thoughts and in my words, in what I have done, and in what I have failed to do.

Parent:

Grant that I may receive you in Holy Communion for the forgiveness of sins,

Response:

and let me be united to you, both here on earth, and forever in Heaven.

All:

Amen.

¡Actividad Familiar 🖉 Divertida!

Esta semana siéntense juntos a decorar un cuaderno para cada miembro de la familia, que puedan usar cada semana en Misa. Anima a cada miembro de la familia a usarlo durante la Misa, para anotar cualquier pensamiento especial o reflexiones sobre las lecturas o la homilía. Los niños pueden dibujar escenas que se estén describiendo en las historias de las Escrituras, para que sean más reales para ellos, o pueden escribir una pequeña oración a Jesús en los momentos de silencio, antes o después de la Comunión. ¡Recuerda mantener esto breve y hacerlo divertido!

¡Oremos Juntos En Familia!

Oración Antes de la Comunión

Papá/Mamá:

Creo, Señor, que eres el Hijo del Dios vivo.

Respuesta:

Creo que viniste al mundo a salvar a los pecadores,

y creo que la Eucaristía es Tu Cuerpo y Sangre.

Papá/Mamá:

Por eso, te ruego que tengas piedad de mí y que perdones los pecados que he cometido,

Respuesta:

de pensamiento, palabra, obra y omisión.

Papá/Mamá:

Permite que pueda recibirte en la Sagrada Comunión, para el perdón de los pecados,

Respuesta:

y permíteme unirme a Ti, tanto en la tierra como por siempre en el cielo.

Todos:

Amén.

Church Scavenger Hunt List

ITEMS:

- ☐ Altar
- ☐ Tabernacle
- ☐ Sanctuary
- ☐ Tabernacle Lamp
- ☐ Ambo
- ☐ Pew
- ☐ Confessional
- ☐ Holy Oils
- ☐ Baptismal Font
- ☐ Crucifix
- ☐ Presider's Chair
- ☐ Paschal Candle
- ☐ Credence Table
- ☐ Mary Statue
- ☐ Statues of Other Saints
- ☐ Stations of the Cross

Flash Cards

Key Words – Session 6

Liturgy

Liturgy of the Mass

Liturgy of the Word

Liturgy of the Eucharist

Lord's Day

Holy Days of Obligation

Flash Cards

Key Words – Session 6 (definitions)

The Liturgy which is comprised of the Liturgy of the Word and the Liturgy of the Eucharist.

The words and actions that we use when we worship God and celebrate the sacraments.

The second part of the Mass in which the bread and wine become the Body and Blood of Christ.

The first part of the Mass in which the Word of God in the readings from Scripture is proclaimed.

Feast days that celebrate special events. Catholics are required to attend Mass on these special days.

Another name for Sunday, because the Lord rose from the dead on a Sunday.

The Liturgy of the Word

☺ Connect — Opening Activity

Jesus Opens the Scriptures

Jesus wants to touch our hearts with his Word in the Bible. When we go to Mass, Jesus is teaching us from the Scriptures, just like he taught his disciples on the road to Emmaus! Place the stickers and color the picture.

Let's Live It

God's Love in the Liturgy

God had a special plan of love for us from the beginning of the world. At Mass, we hear about God's loving plan in the Liturgy of the Word.

Directions: Write the letter of the correct answer in the blanks below.

___ 1. We begin our readings from the Old Testament.

___ 2. We stand and say all the things we believe as Catholics.

___ 3. This reading comes from the New Testament letters.

___ 4. The priest explains the readings to us.

___ 5. The part of the Mass where we hear the Scripture readings.

___ 6. These rites begin the Mass and prepare us for the Liturgy of the Word.

___ 7. We pray to the Lord for our parish, our community, and the world.

___ 8. We sing one of the Psalms.

___ 9. The priest or deacon reads about Jesus's life from the Gospels.

WORD BANK

A. Introductory Rites

B. Liturgy of the Word

C. First Reading

D. Responsorial Psalm

E. Second Reading

F. Gospel

G. Homily

H. Creed

I. Prayers of the Faithful

"In the beginning was the Word, and the Word was with God, and the Word was God."

—John 1:1

Growing the Word in Our Hearts

When we listen to God's Word at Mass, it is like a seed planted in our hearts. We can water and take care of that seed with our love and good actions.

Write on the lines below one or two things you can do to take care of the seed God planted in your heart. Then draw a picture of how that seed will grow into a beautiful plant when you are loving to God and others.

_____

_____

Jesus Said,

"As for [seeds] in the good soil, they are those who, hearing the word, hold it fast in an honest and good heart, and bring forth fruit with patience."

—Luke 8:15

☑ Things We Learned This Week

1. The Mass is one act of worship with two parts: the Liturgy of the Word and the Liturgy of the Eucharist.

2. The first part of the Mass is called the Liturgy of the Word, in which we hear readings from Holy Scripture.

3. After the readings, we pray the Creed, which is a statement of all that we believe as Catholics and is our response of faith to the Word of God.

4. The entire Liturgy of the Word shows God's loving plan of salvation and prepares our hearts for the Liturgy of the Eucharist.

Check out formed.org for free access to reflections on the Sunday Mass readings with *Opening the Word*.

💬 Let's Talk About It

1. Jesus wants us to know how much he loves us, so he teaches us about God's plan each time we go to Mass. What are some things we can do to listen better to the readings at Mass?

2. Talk about your favorite story from the Bible. What does that story mean to you? What do you think God is saying to you?

3. Discuss with your son or daughter some ways that your family can read the Bible more often. Ideas might include keeping a Bible in a special place for all to use.

✝ Let's Read God's Word

The Road to Emmaus – Part 1

The Scripture reading for this week's lesson was from Luke 24:13–27. Please take time to read and reflect on this passage as a family.

95

☑ Lo que aprendimos esta semana:

1. La Misa es un acto de adoración con dos partes: La liturgia de la Palabra y la liturgia de la Eucaristía.

2. La primera parte de la Misa se llama la liturgia de la Palabra, donde escuchamos lecturas de las Sagradas Escrituras.

3. Después de las lecturas, hacemos la oración del Credo, que es una declaración de todo lo que creemos como católicos y es nuestra respuesta de fe a la Palabra de Dios.

4. Toda la liturgia de la Palabra nos muestra el plan amoroso de salvación de Dios y prepara nuestros corazones para la liturgia de la Eucaristía.

✝ Leamos la Palabra de Dios

El Camino a Emaús – Parte 1

La lectura de las Sagradas Escrituras para la lección de esta semana fue del Evangelio de San Lucas 24:13–27. Por favor tomen tiempo para leer y reflexionar sobre este pasaje en familia.

◯ ¡Hablemos Sobre Esto!

1. **Jesús quiere que sepamos cuánto nos ama, así que nos instruye sobre el plan de Dios, cada vez que vamos a Misa y escuchamos las lecturas de la Biblia. ¿Cuáles son algunas cosas que podemos hacer para escuchar más atentamente las lecturas en la Misa?**

2. **Platica sobre tu historia favorita de la Biblia. ¿Qué significa la historia para ti? ¿Qué crees que Dios te está diciendo en esa historia de las Escrituras?**

3. **Habla con tu hijo(a) sobre algunas formas en que tu familia podría leer la Biblia más seguido. Algunas ideas pueden ser: tener una Biblia en un lugar especial para que todos la usen, buscar algún recurso o alguna aplicación en línea, que muestre las lecturas diarias de las Sagradas Escrituras.**

Family Fun Activity

This week we talked about God's Word taking root in our hearts like a seed in fertile soil. A fun activity to do this week is to plant your "seeds of faith!" First, go to the store and buy a small clay pot and some soil and a packet of seeds. Make sure to decorate the pot with your child while you discuss how we need to make our hearts like good soil by listening to the Word of God at Mass and paying attention. This will help your child truly understand that this is a symbol of the fertile soil of your family's faith and the seeds are a symbol of God's Word taking root in your hearts. What a fun way to bring this lesson to life, as you watch your plant grow just like your faith!

Our Family Prays Together

The Apostles' Creed

I believe in God,

the Father almighty,

Creator of heaven and earth,

and in Jesus Christ, his only Son, our Lord,

who was conceived by the Holy Spirit,

born of the Virgin Mary,

suffered under Pontius Pilate,

was crucified, died and was buried;

he descended into hell;

on the third day he rose again from the dead;

he ascended into heaven,

and is seated at the right hand of God the Father almighty;

from there he will come to judge the living and the dead.

I believe in the Holy Spirit,

the holy catholic Church,

the communion of saints,

the forgiveness of sins,

the resurrection of the body,

and life everlasting.

Amen.

¡Actividad Familiar 🖊 Divertida!

Esta semana se habló de la Palabra de Dios que nace en nuestros corazones, como la semilla en tierra fértil. Para entenderlo mejor, esta semana compren una pequeña maceta de barro, tierra y semillas. Decoren juntos la maceta. Explícale a tu hijo(a) que, de la misma forma, necesitamos tener nuestros corazones como una tierra fértil (fe en nuestro hogar), al escuchar la Palabra de Dios en la Misa y poniendo atención. La semilla es símbolo de la Palabra de Dios que echa raíz en nuestros corazones.

¡Así la lección se entenderá mejor al observar la planta crecer, al igual que nuestra fe!

✋ ¡Oremos Juntos En Familia!

El Credo

Creo en Dios, Padre Todopoderoso,

Creador del cielo y de la tierra.

Creo en Jesucristo, su único Hijo, Nuestro Señor,

que fue concebido por obra y gracia del Espíritu Santo,

nació de Santa María Virgen,

padeció bajo el poder de Poncio Pilato

fue crucificado, muerto y sepultado,

descendió a los infiernos,

al tercer día resucitó de entre los muertos,

subió a los cielos

y está sentado a la derecha de Dios, Padre todopoderoso.

Desde allí ha de venir a juzgar a vivos y muertos.

Creo en el Espíritu Santo,

la santa Iglesia Católica,

la comunión de los santos,

el perdón de los pecados,

la resurrección de la carne

y la vida eterna.

Amén.

Flash Cards

Key Words – Session 7

Introductory Rites

Entrance Antiphon

Sign of the Cross

Penitential Act

Gloria

Collect

Flash Cards

Key Words – Session 7 (definitions)

The song that is sung as the priest enters the church for Mass.

The part of the Mass that comes before the Liturgy of the Word.

The prayer in which we tell God we are sorry for our sins and ask for his mercy.

A large cross that is traced from forehead to chest and from left shoulder to right shoulder.

The special prayer that the priest prays at the end of the Introductory Rite.

The ancient hymn of praise that we sing to God the Father, God the Son, and God the Holy Spirit at Mass.

Flash Cards

Key Words – Session 7

Liturgy of the Word	First Reading
Responsorial Psalm	Second Reading
Epistles	Alleluia

Flash Cards

Key Words – Session 7 (definitions)

Readings at Mass, usually from the Old Testament. In it we hear about God's plan for salvation.

The readings from Scripture and their explanation.

The reading after the Responsorial Psalm from the Letters of the New Testament.

The psalm we sing together after the First Reading.

The chant sung before the Gospel is read meaning "Praise the Lord."

The letters written to the early Church.

Flash Cards

Key Words – Session 7

Gospel

Homily

Creed / Profession of Faith

Prayer of the Faithful

Flash Cards

Key Words – Session 7 (definitions)

An explanation of the readings, given by the priest or deacon.

The reading from one of the four Gospels, telling us about the life of Christ.

Prayers of intercession, for our parish, community, and the world.

Our response of faith to the Word of God we heard in the readings.

The Liturgy of the Eucharist

😊 Connect — Opening Activity

Breaking Bread

After Jesus met the two disciples on the road to Emmaus, he broke the bread and gave them the Eucharist. They knew he was Jesus then because he broke bread with them. Place the sticker and color the picture.

Let's Live It

The Mass Sends Us on a Mission

Write the letter of the correct answer in the blanks below. Then use the letters of the correct answers to fill in the meaning of the word *Mass*.

The word "Mass" means:

___ ___ ___ ___ ___ ___ ___ ___
1.   2.   3.   4.   5.   6.   7.   8.

The Mass sends us into the world to tell others about Jesus.

1. ___ In the Liturgy of the _____, Jesus becomes present to us, Body, Blood, Soul, and Divinity.
   S. Word   T. Eucharist   U. Communion

2. ___ The Liturgy of the Eucharist begins with the Presentation of the _____, when the bread and wine are offered to God.
   M. People   N. Word   O. Gifts

3. ___ The _____ is the prayer when we sing "Holy, holy, holy . . ."
   B. Sanctus   C. Preface   D. Lord's Prayer

4. ___ The words of _____ change the bread and wine into the Body and Blood of Christ.
   C. faith   D. truth   E. consecration

5. ___ The Eucharistic Prayer ends with the Great _____.
   R. Hooray   S. Amen   T. Surprise

6. ___ After the Lord's Prayer, we have the _____ ____ _____, when we say, "Peace be with you" to those around us.
   E. Sign of Peace   F. Lamb of God   G. End of Mass

7. ___ We go forward to receive Jesus in Holy _____.
   L. Supper   M. Mealtime   N. Communion

8. ___ The Concluding Rite is when the priest gives us a blessing, and we are sent into the world to _____ the Good News.
   T. spread   U. block   V. forget

The Love of Jesus

At the end of Mass, the priest always blesses us and sends us out to bring Christ's love to the world. Write on the lines below one or two things you can do to bring the love of Jesus to others. Then draw a picture showing one thing that you would like to start doing this week.

_____

_____

Jesus Said,

"Love one another as I have loved you."

—John 15:12

☑ Things We Learned This Week

1. The Mass is one act of worship with two parts: the Liturgy of the Word and the Liturgy of the Eucharist.

2. The second part of the Mass is called the Liturgy of the Eucharist, where Jesus becomes present to us, Body, Blood, Soul, and Divinity.

3. Jesus's sacrifice on the Cross and his Resurrection are made present to us, and we also offer our lives as living sacrifices to God.

4. When we receive Holy Communion, we are united with Jesus in a very special way.

5. The Mass sends us forth to spread the Gospel by the witness of our lives.

🔍 Let's Talk About It

1. Just as Jesus's friends truly saw him in the breaking of the bread, he wants us to see him in the Eucharist too! How is the Eucharist the greatest sign of God's love for us and his desire that we will be close to him always?

2. Talk about your favorite part of the Mass. What makes that special to you? How does that part of the Mass make you feel close to Jesus?

3. Discuss some ways that your family can bring Jesus's love to the world. What can you do in your community, your work, or your school to spread the love of Christ to others?

📖 Let's Read God's Word

The Road to Emmaus – Part 2

The Scripture reading for this week's lesson was from Luke 24:28–35. Please take time to read and reflect on this passage as a family.

☑ Lo que aprendimos esta semana:

1. La Misa es un acto de adoración con dos partes: la liturgia de la Palabra y la liturgia de la Eucaristía.

2. La segunda parte de la Misa se llama la liturgia de la Eucaristía, donde Jesús se hace presente, en Cuerpo, Sangre, Alma y Divinidad.

3. El sacrificio de Jesús en la cruz se hace presente, y nosotros también ofrecemos nuestras vidas como un sacrificio vivo a Dios.

4. Cuando recibimos la Sagrada Comunión, nos unimos a Jesús en una forma muy especial.

5. La Misa nos envía a proclamar el Evangelio, siendo testigos con nuestras vidas.

⟲ ¡Hablemos Sobre Esto!

1. ¡Así como los amigos de Jesús verdaderamente lo reconocieron al partir el pan, Él desea que lo veamos también en la Eucaristía! ¿Cómo la Eucaristía es el signo más grande del amor de Dios por nosotros y Su deseo de que estemos siempre cerca de Él?

2. Platica sobre tu parte favorita de la Misa. ¿Qué la hace especial para ti? ¿Cómo esa parte de la Misa te hace sentir cerca de Jesús?

3. Platiquen de algunas maneras en que tu familia puede llevar el amor de Jesús al mundo. ¿Qué pueden hacer en su comunidad, en tu propio trabajo, o en la escuela, para transmitir el amor de Cristo a los demás?

Leamos la Palabra de Dios

El Camino a Emaús – Parte 2

La lectura de las Sagradas Escrituras para la lección de esta semana fue del Evangelio de San Lucas 24:28–35. Por favor tomen tiempo para leer y reflexionar sobre este pasaje en familia.

Family Fun Activity

As your child's First Holy Communion Day approaches, take some time to look back at pictures from other family members' First Communions. Share special memories you have of the first time you received Jesus and the celebration of that special day. Then be sure to talk about what your family will do to celebrate your child's special day soon! It would also be a good idea to practice with your child how to receive so they are not nervous and feel prepared to receive Jesus in this very special way.

Our Family Prays Together

The Anima Christi

(A traditional prayer after Communion)

Soul of Christ, sanctify me.

Body of Christ, save me.

Blood of Christ, inebriate me.

Water from the side of Christ, wash me.

Passion of Christ, strengthen me.

O good Jesus, hear me.

Within your wounds, conceal me.

Do not permit me to be parted from you.

From the evil foe, protect me.

At the hour of my death, call me.

And bid me come to you,

to praise you with all your saints

for ever and ever.

Amen.

Explore the Faith Together

For more information on Catholic traditions and teachings as well as Catholic movies, books, audios, and more, please check out formed.org. Ask your Director of Religious Education if your parish has a subscription to log on for free!

¡Actividad Familiar Divertida!

Esta semana es nuestra semana final en preparación para la Primera Comunión de tu hijo(a). Dedica tiempo para ver las fotos de Primeras Comuniones de otros familiares. Comparte las memorias especiales que tienes de la primera vez que recibiste a Jesús y la celebración de ese día tan especial. ¡Luego asegúrate de hablar sobre lo que hará tu familia para celebrar el día especial de tu hijo(a) que se acerca! Sería también buena idea practicar con tu hijo(a) cómo recibir la comunión para que no esté nervioso(a) y se sienta preparado(a) para recibir a Jesús en esta forma tan especial.

¡Oremos Juntos En Familia!

Alma de Cristo

(Una oración tradicional para después de la Comunión)

Alma de Cristo, santifícame.

Cuerpo de Cristo, sálvame.

Sangre de Cristo, embriágame.

Agua del costado de Cristo, lávame.

Pasión de Cristo, confórtame.

Oh buen Jesús, óyeme.

Dentro de tus llagas, escóndeme.

No permitas que me separe de Ti.

Del maligno enemigo, defiéndeme.

En la hora de mi muerte, llámame.

Y mándame ir a Ti,

para que, con Tus santos, Te alabe y Te bendiga,

por los siglos de los siglos. Amén.

Exploren Juntos La Fe

Para más información acerca de las tradiciones y enseñanzas católicas, y para encontrar material católico como películas, libros, audios, etc., puedes checar la página formed.org. ¡Pregúntale al director de educación religiosa si tu parroquia tiene un código parroquial para tener acceso gratuito!

Flash Cards

Key Words – Session 8

Presentation of the Gifts

Preparation of the Altar

Prayer over the Offerings

The Eucharistic Prayer

Preface

Sanctus

Flash Cards

Key Words – Session 8 (definitions)

The priest or deacon prepares the altar by placing all the necessary items in their places.

The bread and wine are brought up to the priest.

The center and high point of the Liturgy of the Eucharist.

The prayer the priest prays over the bread and wine after they have been placed on the altar.

The song we all sing in union with the hosts of Heaven: "Holy, holy, holy."

The first part of the Eucharistic Prayer, in which the priest gives thanks and glory to God.

Flash Cards

Key Words – Session 8

Epiclesis

Institution Narrative

Words of Consecration

The Mystery of Faith or Memorial Acclamation

Chalice

Paten

Flash Cards

Key Words – Session 8 (definitions)

The part of the Eucharistic Prayer that tells the story of the Last Supper.	When the priest extends his hands over the bread and wine and asks the Holy Spirit to come down so that they may be changed into the Body and Blood of Christ.
In this prayer we remember the Passion, Death, and Resurrection of Jesus, and express our faith that he will come again.	"This is my Body..." and "This is the chalice of my Blood..."
The special plate that holds the Host.	The special cup that holds the wine that will become the Blood of Christ.

Flash Cards

Key Words – Session 8

Doxology

Great Amen

The Communion Rite

Lamb of God

Holy Communion

Prayer after Communion

Flash Cards

Key Words – Session 8 (definitions)

The "amen" that the whole congregation says or sings in response to the Doxology.

The prayer of praise giving glory to God at the end of the Eucharistic Prayer, which the priest prays while elevating the chalice.

The prayer we say or sing together, which begins "Lamb of God, you take away the sins of the world, have mercy on us…"

We pray the Lord's Prayer together.

The prayer the priest says after we have all received Holy Communion.

The time when we receive the Body and Blood of our Lord under the appearance of bread and wine.

Flash Cards

Key Words – Session 8

Concluding Rite

In persona Christi Capitis

Flash Cards

Key Words – Session 8 (definitions)

In the Mass, the priest acts "in the Person of Jesus the Head," as the representative of Jesus.

The priest gives us a final blessing, and we all make the Sign of the Cross. Then the priest or deacon announces that the Mass has ended.